Turtles and Hatchlings

by Ann-Marie Kishel

first step nonfiction

Lerner Publications · Minneapolis

A turtle has a shell.

A hatchling has a shell.

A turtle has a neck.

A hatchling has a neck.

A turtle has legs.

A hatchling has legs.

Turtles and hatchlings
are alike.